AN INTRODUCTION TO MAPPERLEY PARK

Part One

The Park Estate, Nottingham, is essentially Victorian in concept and execution. In January 1854 T C Hine, the pre-eminent Nottingham architect of the day, was appointed by the 5th Duke of Newcastle to the Surveyship of the Duke's Park Estate. Hine's spacious design of the late 1850s exploited much of the Park's natural configuration giving the area an irresistible appeal to the successful prosperous business and professional townsmen! By the mid 1890s very few prime sites remained, thus the Edwardian content of the Park is slight, virtually restricted to a few plots on the eastern roads and several on Huntingdon Drive. In contrast, the heart of Mapperley Park is Edwardian. Some roads were laid out prior to 1877, the year the town of Nottingham substantially increased in size from 1,996 to 10,935 acres through the Borough Extension Act. Mapperley, Carrington and Sherwood, formerly in the Parish of Basford, were among a number of satellite villages thus brought within the compass of the town. The main purpose of a map prepared by the Borough Engineer, Marriott Ogle Tarbotton, published in 1877, was to show the nature and alignment of the drainage and sewerage system(s) of the town and adjoining areas prior to expansion. Fortunately for the historian the map also shows roads existing by, say, 1876. On this map Red Hill Lane and Red Lane (Redcliffe Road), a short Zulla Road leading to Magdala Road, Lucknow Road and the beginnings of Lucknow Drive are all named. From the passing of the Act until the turn of the century more roads were set out and some building took place, this development being limited to the area from Redcliffe Road extending northwards to a line broadly linking Lucknow Avenue (east) and Ebers Road (west).

Nevertheless, the essential atmosphere, especially in the northern area with its generous yet manageable houses, relates to a world oblivious of European intrigues and an impending world war. There is something wistfully splendid about Mapperley Park when illuminated by the late evening sun, its houses seemingly on terraces, dropping from heights close to Woodborough Road and levelling out to the lower Mansfield Road.

Mapperley Park lacked the presence of an aristocratic family and the associated flamboyance, arrogance and real wealth. Wrights, even as successful bankers, are not really Newcastles. Mapperley Park's transformation from a mixture of open parkland, rich meadows and a little arable land into a select planned Edwardian suburb is relatively uneventful. The progressive stages of its evolution are reasonably well served by reliable maps from a variety of sources.

The early history of the area has been related in some detail by Stapleton in his 'Old Mapperley' published in 1902, and although more recent work might alter the details this remains the standard reference. Most of its contents lie outside this narrative. Stapleton quotes an advertisement from the Nottingham Journal of 14 November 1772 and that provides a good starting point.

> "To be sold to the best bidder together, or in several lots at the house of Mr Semes, the Blackmoor's Head, in Nottingham, on Thursday the 7th day of January next, between the hours of eleven and four, subject to such conditions as shall be then produced, unless sold in the meantime by private contract, of which timely notice will be given in this paper: A Compact freehold estate called Mapperley situate in the parish of Basford, within one mile of Nottingham, consisting of two messuage houses, and 18 closes of rich meadow and

pasture land adjoining thereto, and lying within a ring fence, containing 88 acres and upwards. There are also 12 acres of arable land to the said estate, as its proportion of Break from the Forest. Mapperley is a very pleasant situation, near Sherwood Forest, in a fine sporting country and is entitled to common right, without stint on the said Forest."

Part of Chapman's Map of Nottinghamshire 1774 showing the open nature of the area around Mapperley. The two black squares could be the ".... two messuage houses" of the 1773 sale.

This is the estate shown on the first large scale map of Nottinghamshire, that was surveyed by John Chapman in 1774 and published in 1776. John Smith, the banker, is the most likely purchaser of the estate, he died in 1776. One of his three daughters, Mary, was married to Thomas Wright and by a deed of partition dated 20 May 1977 they were apportioned the Mapperley and Basford estates. Thomas died in 1790 and he was succeeded by his eldest son, Ichabod, then aged 23.

As a result of the Basford Inclosure Act of 1792, not only was the old central portion of the Park awarded to the Wright family, but also all the land from Redcliffe Road to what is now Private [2] Road and from roughly the present Woodborough Road to the Mansfield Road. Mapperley Hall was built about this time, an extra floor was added c 1845 when Italianate details were added to the west front. The Hall was extended and altered by the Nottingham Architects Robert Evans and William Jolley in 1889-90. Earlier in 1885 they designed the entrance lodge at the end of the drive to the Hall, this survives on the corner of Mapperley Hall Drive and Mansfield Road. About 1794 Ichabod enclosed the outer park and started a plantation of mixed trees: oak, ash, elm, beech, etc., some survived to the 1920s.

Cross Road

Henry Cavendish Esquire for Tithes.

120

Ichabod Wright Esq

175
Wm Smith

Mansfield Turnpike Road

fry Brock

185
Duke of Newcastle

Thos Caunt 176
Francis Evans Esq 176a

184

Wright Esquire

178
F.&F. James
179
Thos Hill
177
Jas Evans Exors

180
Jas Sturt
181
Jno Evans Esq

Ichabod

119

182
Francis Read

Duke of Newcastle

Rt Smith Esq
183

from Nottingham

Mapperley Hills Road

N   O   T   T   I   N   G

Red Lane

M A H G

from Nottingham

Part of the Basford Inclosure Map 1792. Notice the land allocated to Ichabod Wright, the Duke of Newcastle (especially 185) and R Smith Esq (183).

Until the enlargement of the borough in 1877 the northern boundary between the town and the parish of Basford lay in part along the line of Redcliffe Road or, as it was earlier and aptly known, Red Lane. The Mansfield Road as it leaves Nottingham runs very close to the junction of the Bunter Sandstone to the west and the Keuper Marl to the east. Red Lane came down to the Mansfield road through high clay banks, its surface was very bad and it was usually impassable in winter. Alderman William Burgass had a brickyard at Mapperley and to avoid transportation problems in winter, he moved his bricks during the summer and stockpiled them on waste ground near what is now the junction of Mansfield Road and Gregory Boulevard. In addition, of course, carts could not get coal up to the kilns during the winter months.

As a result of the passing of the Mansfield Turnpike Ace of 1787 the first five miles from Nottingham to Rufford became improved to turnpike standards and thus attracted coach and four traffic. Prior to that, as can be seen from Chapman's map, the road from Gallows Hill (Forest Road East) to Swine House Road (Woodthorpe Drive) there were no fields or hedges. Indeed, on both sides of the road at Gallows Hill there were exposed caves, said to be the haunt of highwaymen.[3]

Mapperley Road was cut but not paved and Woodborough Road was improved from a foot and bridge track in the early 1850s. Even then until properly made-up they were bedeviled with deep clay ruts. Thus the early importance of Red Lane, even as only a cart track, can be appreciated when it is realised that the next road up to Mapperley 'top' was Swine House Road, later Scout Lane, and now Woodthorpe Drive. Token improvement had been carried out from time to time usually in the guise of work created for the relief of the poor. In 1837 Red Lane, among others, was partly levelled and repaired, a few years later Mapperley Hills received attention.

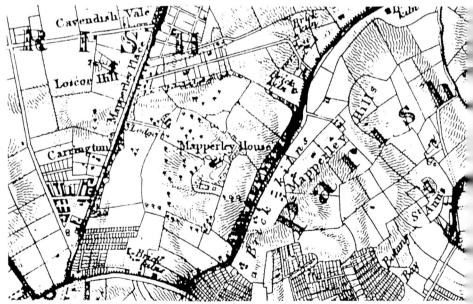

Part of Sanderson's Map '20 Miles Around Mansfield' 1835-6. Notice the allotment gardens south of Carrington; Mapperley House and its trees; and Mapperley Place.

The results of enclosure are well shown on George Sanderson's map '20 Miles Around Mansfield' (1835). A definite field pattern is shown as well as the Carrington model settlement[4], the Mapperley Place Estate and the establishment of a number of allotments or gardens in the southwest corner of the Mapperley lands. A map of 'Mapperley Hall Estate near Nottingham, the Property of I C Wright Esq' was prepared by Frederick Jackson of Nottingham and published in 1863. The fields and plots of the estate are numbered as if for an inventory or perhaps for an auction.

It is interesting to speculate at this point on the intentions of the Wright family to dispose of their Mapperley Estate. The great Nottingham Enclosure of 1845 was officially completed in 1865 although most of the land in the Sandfield had been apportioned well before this time. The Arboretum area had developed into a desirable suburb. The expansion of Nottingham to absorb its neighbouring parishes was first considered officially in October 1871. Then the council appointed a committee .... "to prepare a Bill of a general character for the improvement of the Borough." A much amended and pruned General Improvement Bill was presented in 1873 and passed in 1874. The enlargement of boundaries of the town, however, were obtained in a new Bill deposited in Parliament 13 December 1876 and which received Royal Assent on 11 June 1877; the 'Nottingham Borough Extension Act[5]." Thus it was probably advisable to wait for the opportune time to come on the market. The southern portion of the Estate would provide good sites not so far from the centre of town and would receive the benefits of services provided by an ambitious big town.

There might be a much more mundane explanation for the 1863 map. The Ichabod Wright who built Mapperley Hall died in 1862 in his 96th year; he had ten daughters and three sons. Ichabod Charles, the eldest son, died in 1871 aged 76. So perhaps it was a matter of inheritance.

Notes:

1   This contrasted with P F Robinson's regimented Regency layout of 1827 which was greatly influenced by Nash's grand London Squares. Robinson seems blissfully to have ignored the Park's topography. That this ill considered plan was abandoned can in part be considered an unexpected bonus resulting from the firing of Nottingham Castle in October 1831.

2   By the Basford Enclosure Act the Duke of Newcastle was awarded the strip of land on which Private Road now stands. This land was developed as the Mapperley Place Estate and was owned by Samuel Cartledge who insisted that the houses built should be stone coloured and slated. The old cottage called 'Mapperley Place' is thought to have been erected about 1825. Private Road and Mapperley Street had been formed by 1835 (Sanderson's map). White's Nottinghamshire Director 1832) states: "Mapperley Place two miles north of Nottingham is another range of modern villas partly upon Mansfield Road and extending eastwards." On the 'Private Road' nine voters were listed in the Poll Book of 1832. Nearby, through enclosure, Henry Cavendish was awarded a piece of land for 'tithes' hence the name Cavendish Hill for a portion of Mansfield Road and Cavendish Vale in Sherwood.

BEAUTIFUL SITUATIONS

FOR THE ERECTION OF

COUNTRY RESIDENCES,

(FREEHOLD AND TITHE FREE)

In the immediate Vicinity of Nottingham.

—•◆•—

TO BE SOLD BY AUCTION,

By Mr. SCOTT,

At the Spread Eagle Inn, Nottingham, on Wednesday the 14th Day of August next, at Three o'Clock in the Afternoon, in Lots conveniently laid out, WITHOUT ANY RESTRICTIONS (upon such Conditions as will be produced at the Time of Sale),

A Most beautiful and valuable TRACT of LAND, Freehold and Tithe-free, within a short distance of the Town of Nottingham, adjoining the London Turnpike Road leading to Mansfield; bounded on both Sides by the Estates of Ichabod Wright, Esq. and James Hooley, Esq. in the Parish of Basford, in the County of Nottingham, called

MAPPERLEY PLACE.

The Land is divided into Lots, suitable for the erection of Houses intended for Country Residences; and either with or without Gardens and Pleasure Grounds; and affords the most favourable Opportunity ever offered to the Public for that purpose in the Vicinity of Nottingham.

The Scenery commands the most extensive and beautiful Views which the Neighbourhood of Nottingham presents, comprising, towards the West, WOLLATON HALL and PARK, NUTTALL TEMPLE, extending to Watnall and Annesley; and towards the East and South, BELVOIR CASTLE and the Leicestershire Hills; with the intermediate Scenery, extending over the rich and woody Vale of TRENT, the Woods of COLWICK, WILFORD, and CLIFTON.

The Lots will be supplied with Water at a very moderate Expense, and Purchasers may be accommodated with a few Acres of Land to rent, on reasonable Terms.

The Purchasers will be entitled to Votes for the County of Nottingham.

A Brick Yard is erected at the extremity of the Estate for supplying Purchasers, at a reasonable Rate, with Bricks for Building.

Further Particulars may be known, and Plans of the Property may be seen at the Office of Mr. ALLSOPP, Solicitor; at the House of Mr. SCOTT, Auctioneer, Nottingham; and at the Lodge on the Estate.

—••◉•—

MAPPERLEY PLACE, IN LOTS.

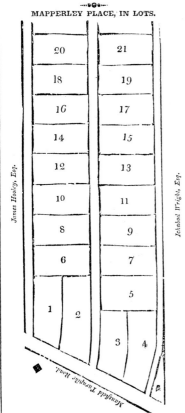

BEAUTIFUL SITUATIONS

FOR THE ERECTION OF

COUNTRY RESIDENCES,

(FREEHOLD AND TITHE FREE)

IN THE IMMEDIATE VICINITY OF NOTTINGHAM.

—•◆•—

To be SOLD by PRIVATE CONTRACT,

THE remaining Lots of a most beautiful and valuable TRACT of LAND, that were not sold at the Auction on the 14th instant, Freehold and Tithe free, within a short distance of the Town of Nottingham, adjoining the London Turnpike Road leading to Mansfield; bounded on both Sides by the Estates of Ichabod Wright, Esq. and James Hooley, Esq. in the Parish of Basford, in the County of Nottingham, called

Mapperley Place.

The Land is divided into Lots, suitable for the erection of Houses intended for Country Residences; and either with or without Gardens and Pleasure Grounds; and affords the most favourable Opportunity ever afforded to the Public for that purpose in the Vicinity of Nottingham.

The Scenery commands the most extensive and beautiful Views which the Neighbourhood of Nottingham presents, comprising, towards the West, WOLLATON HALL and PARK, NUTTALL TEMPLE, extending to Watnall and Annesley; and towards the East and South, BELVOIR CASTLE and the Leicestershire Hills; with the intermediate Scenery, extending over the rich and woody Vale of TRENT, the Woods of COLWICK, WILFORD, and CLIFTON.

The Lots will be supplied with Water at a very moderate Expense, and Purchasers may be accommodated with a few Acres of Land to rent, on reasonable Terms.

The Purchasers will be entitled to Votes for the County of Nottingham.

A Brick Yard is erected at the extremity of the Estate for supplying Purchasers, at a reasonable Rate, with Bricks for Building.

Further Particulars may be known, and Plans of the Property may be seen at the Office of Mr. ALLSOPP, Solicitor; at the House of Mr. SCOTT, Auctioneer, Nottingham; and at the Lodge on the Estate.

Advertisements in the Nottingham Journal 2nd / 9th and 17th / 24th August 1822 for the sale of Mapperley Place.
It is likely that the plans were prepared by Henry Moses Wood the Nottingham architect and surveyor.

MAPPERLY HOUSE.

Ichabod Wright, Esq, banker

MAPPERLY PLACE.	SHERWOOD HILL.
Brazier Mrs. F. lace maker	Clarke John, gentleman
Calvert Wm. lace maker	Cox Edward, liquor merchant
Dale Rich., ale & porter merch.	Forman Capt. Geo., 56th Regt
Hall John, gent.	foot
Maltby Thomas, gent.	Gibson Lucy, gentlewoman
Nightingale R. tailor	Newball Thomas, gentleman
Sanders Miss H. gentlewoman	Shaw Wm. Drury, gentleman
Taylor Thomas, cotton bobbin manufacturer	Whitlark John, lace manufac.
Taylor John, schoolmaster	Willey Samuel, lace maker
Tibbutt John, lace manufac.	
Schenck John, lace manufac.	

Entry in Dearden's Directory of 1834.

3   In c 1856 according to the Nottingham Date Book, whilst the church cemetery was under construction a number of caves showing evidence of habitation were uncovered. In clearing out these caves "rough looking pistols, small crowbars, and similar weapons, evidence long buried and completely corroded" were discovered. The last execution at Gallows Hill took place on 2 April 1827. It was for highway robbery.

4   Carrington model settlement. The Basford Enclosure Act allocated the six acres at the junction of the Mansfield and Hucknall roads to Robert Smith, MP - later Lord Carrington, principal partner in the London branch of Smith's Bank. The land was sold to Ichabod Wright who divided it into building plots, laid out streets and created its triangular market place early in the nineteenth century.

5   The Nottingham Borough Extension Act 1877 increased the area of the town from 1,996 acres to 10,935 acres and the population from 86,621 (1871 census) to about 157,000. The parishes of Basford (which included Mapperley Park), Bulwell, Lenton, Radford, Sneinton and Wilford became suburbs of a larger Nottingham.

The Parish of Basford taken from a map of Nottingham: "Corporation of Nottingham, Proposed Borough Extension, Session 1876-77."

Prepared by S.G. Johnson, Town Clerk and M. Ogle Tarbotton, Borough Engineer, the map was at a scale of 2 1/4 inches to 1 mile. The area of Basford Parish was given as 2,720 acres, its estimated population as 14,500 (13,038 at the 1871 census) and a rateable value of £40,512.

Carrington and the Wright family's Mapperley Estate on the map of the greater Nottingham area by M O Tarbotton, the Borough surveyor/engineer, 1877

Part Two

Ichabod Wright was a successful banker, as early as 1794 he became a partner in the bank founded by his grandfather in 1760 on Long Row. Throughout his long life he led the 'Wrights' through the crises that toppled less secure institutions. He saw the bank establish itself in Swine Green in 1795 (Carlton Street from c 1810). He was well respected in Nottingham and beyond. He became a Freeman of the town in 1791. Ichabod, like the rest of the Wright family, maintained an interest in the flourishing hamlet of Carrington - almost overlooked by the family seat and which he, in effect, helped to create. In 1833 he gave land at the corner of Selkirk Street for the proposed Carrington National Schools and the family gave over £300 of the £700 needed for the building. In 1841 the site of St John's, Carrington, was donated by Ichabod and the family contributed almost £2,000 towards the cost of the church, designed by William Surplice of Nottingham, and its endowment.[1] In 1840 General Sir Charles James Napier was Commander of troops in the Northern Counties and had his headquarters in Wheeler Gate, Nottingham. He skilfully cooled down the potential heat of local Chartist activity, he was full of praise for the philanthropy of the Wrights. "There is one family here that would save a city from God's wrath, Wrights the bankers." Ichabod was indeed a hard man to follow. His eldest son, Ichabod Charles, had been made a joint manager of the bank in 1825, and later became a partner, but he only outlived his father by some nine years.

A survey and valuation of the Mapperley Park Estate, carried out not long after the death of Ichabod Wright in 1862, was completed by March 1863. Ichabod Charles appears to have remained at the Hall until c 1869. An inventory of the fixtures of Mapperley Hall was compiled and completed by August 1869. On 25 August 1869 he agreed to lease the Hall and its grounds to Edward Manlove of Ruddington.[2] Under this contract Manlove had the use of "... Mapperley Hall, gardens, pleasure grounds, etc. (7 acres, 3 roods, 36 perches) pasture land the approach road (13 acres, 3 roods, 26 perches) use of pond and ornamental plantation, Lodge or Barn Close (6 acres, 1 rood, 36 perchest); Lodge at gate adjoining Mansfield turnpike road; also all fixtures and articles specified in attached inventory.[3] Two bedrooms reserved out of lease for leaser's storages for 7 years at £231-11-0d per annum. [He] Covenants to spend £150 on repairs in the first year, to paint, maintain and keep in repair, to keep up gardens, hothouses, conservatories, etc, to cultivate and dress grassland, to fell no timber."

Ichabod Charles Wright died in 1871 aged 76 at Heathfield Hall, Sussex, the home of his son, Colonel Charles Ichabod Wright. Colonel Wright, of the 'Robin Hoods', was elected MP for Nottingham in November 1868, but after 15 months ill health forced him to apply for the Chiltern Hundreds. He took up residence at Stapleford Hall.

He was still there on 16 February 1877 when he leased Mapperley Hall to William Lambert[4], co-leasers were Henry Smith Wright of Lenton Hall[5] and Frederick Wright of Radcliffe-on-Trent. The existing lease was surrendered from the Wrights to Lambert who received thereby "... Mapperley Hall with grounds, pleasure gardens and lands and use of contents as listed in appended inventory for 19 years at £560 per annum". [He] "Covenants to paint, maintain, keep

PLAN OF MAPPERLEY PARK ESTATE
c 1875 by Robert Evans and William Jolley

SCALE OF CHAINS

The Southern Part of the Mapperley Estate c 1879
The 'Basford' Gardens survive on this OS map but
probably not in reality!

up gardens, hothouses, etc, cultivate land, fell no timber." Lambert, in fact, stayed only about ten years at the Hall, by 1888 he had moved to Lenton Firs.

Meanwhile, Colonel Wright started to release land on that southern part of the estate excluded from the leasing arrangements. The first available evidence of the impending breakup of the estate is in a document dated 15 December 1873.

> "Sale conditions Mapperley Park Estate, with building restrictions, etc and agreement by William Windley of Nottingham, Esq., to purchase 5 acres, 3 roods, 5 perches bounded on three sides by Woodborough Road, Magdala Road and Lucknow Drive on which only six houses to be built for £7,695." (Plan - missing)

The reference here to Magdala Road and Lucknow Drive is interesting for it does suggest that some kind of development plan had been prepared, possibly by the Nottingham architectural partnership of Robert Evans and William Jolley. At this time the area was in Basford Parish, it came within the town of Nottingham after the 1877 Act. Thus although Building Plans had to be deposited from September 1874[6] in the town, any development north of Red Lane (Redcliffe Road) would not be submitted to the town's officials until after 1877.

There is no evidence that Windley immediately proceeded to develop his part of the estate. The first mention of Magdala Road occurring in the Nottingham Building Applications is on 26 September 1879 when a "Plan and Section of Upper Portion of Magdala Road", Windley's end, although he died in 1877, received approval. The application was made by Evans and Jolley acting for a young surveyor, Arthur R Calvert, who had just left their office to start his own practice. On this plan Lucknow Road and Lucknow Drive are shown. Evans and Jolley produced a generalised "Plan of Mapperley Park Estate which although not dated has always been assumed to be c 1880. No new named roads are shown on it but the gardens north of Red Lane are named twice. This plan must be of an earlier date, for as noted the Tarbotton map, printed in 1877, has roads clearly drawn in and named at the southern end of the estate. Evans and Jolley together with Calvert, later prepared the plans and sections of all the roads on the southern part of the estate. With one exception all of the intended road schemes were undertaken for Messrs Wright, Evans and Jolley; and Calvert, also submitted plans for roads on the other side of Mansfield Road, north of St John's Church, Carrington; the Loscoe Hill Estate (1879-82) and moving into Sherwood, the Woodville Estate (1879)."

The extensive gardens, sometimes known as the Basford gardens, which were situated on the eastern side of Mansfield Road from about the line of the present Magdala Road to a point almost opposite the New Inn, survived until the mid 1870s. Then the tenants of these gardens received from C I Wright, H Smith Wright and F Wright a printed notice to quit, thus allowing development to commence.

It is puzzling that Tarbotton's map has no drawn evidence of the gardens but the Ordnance Survey map of 1881 - no doubt surveyed earlier - shows them in some detail. Tarbotton in fact appears to suggest a start had been made on dividing up the land at the western end of Red Lane close to Mansfield Road, into building plots. Evans and Jolley, and Tarbotton have a similar large field located alongside Mansfield Road facing St John's Church. Only Tarbotton has drawn in the Cricket Ground. Whose cricket ground was it? Was it for the exclusive use of the Wright family and their house guests or was there a Carrington Cricket Club at this time?"

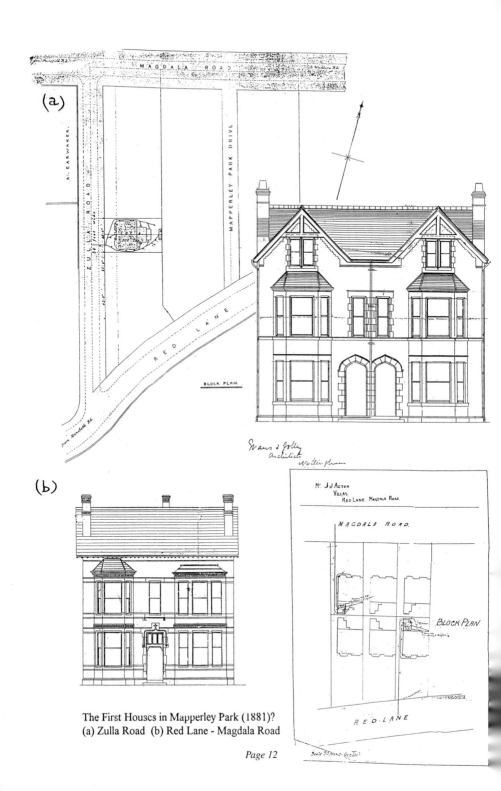

(a)

(b)

The First Houses in Mapperley Park (1881)?
(a) Zulla Road (b) Red Lane - Magdala Road

There appears to be no plan lodged with the town for the lower portion of Magdala Road. Predating the plans for the upper portion are the 'Plans and Section of New Road called Cyprus Road.' These were presented by Evans and Jolley on 7 February 1879. This is somewhat unexpected for Cyprus Road is close to the centre of the estate. This scheme was apparently not pursued for A R Calvert put forward 'Plans and Sections of New Streets off Magdala Road to be called Cyprus Road' on 25 May 1883 and for Lucknow Avenue on 29 June 1883. Evans and Jolley came back on 18 June 1886 with 'Plans and Sections for New Streets: Lucknow Avenue, Cyprus Road, Zulla Road Continuation, for Messrs Wright'. This apparent puzzle is most likely the result of the surveyor(s) failing to appreciate the gradient of the land, the fall from east to west down towards the Mansfield Road and the associated drainage problems. Calvert had three attempts to get his plans for a 'New Road, for Bell and Son, Mapperley Park Drive' linking Red Lane to Magdala Road, approved in June 1881. A question over the level of Mansfield Road brought one disapproval. Zulla Road, which also linked Red Lane with Magdala Road, must date from the mid 1870s. Its extension, initially referred to as Zulla Road North, was first submitted by Calvert on 6 July 1883. Evans and Jolley's first involvement with the Zulla Road extension was on 13 November 1885 when their plans included Shirley Road for the first time. Ebers Road is first mentioned in 1890 on a revised design by A W Brewill for two semi-detached villa residences at the northern end of the newly completed Zulla Road. Some architects pushed, no doubt, by their clients showed great enthusiasm for they submitted house plans before the relevant roads on which they were to stand had been approved. Some houses were certainly under construction before these roads were completed.

The names chosen for these early Mapperley Park roads need some explanation. Several are associated with the campaigns of the British Army in the mid to late 19th century. This is no doubt due to the fact that the Wrights were in part a military family.

The British residency in **Lucknow** was besieged in 1857 during the Indian Mutiny. The city was temporarily relieved by Havelock and Outram on 25 September but had to wait until 17 November for final relief from Colin Campbell.

In January 1868 a British expedition to Ethiopia, led by General Sir Robert Napier, included the 45th Regiment. The army's presence in Ethiopia followed the imprisonment of the British Consul by King Theodore the Third. **Magdala** was the fortress and last stronghold of "mad" Theodore. It was stormed and captured on 13 April 1868. **Zulla** on Annesley Bay, an inlet on the Red Sea coast was the embarkation port for the victorious British Army returning to Bombay.

Cyprus is a puzzle. Through a secret Anglo-Turkish agreement of 4 January 1878 Britain promised to defend Turkey against attack, part of a move to check Russian advances in Asia Minor. As part of this strategy Britain would be allowed to occupy **Cyprus**. Confirmation of this move came when the Treaty of Berlin was signed on 13 July 1878. Is this of sufficient lasting family interest to be perpetuated as an estate road name?

Ebers is even more of a problem. The only suggestions have centred on the German Egyptologist, professor and novelist, Georg Moritz **Ebers**, 1837-98. If he was the link, was he admired, enjoyed as a novelist (in translation!) or lecturer; or was he a friend of the more learned members of the family?

As the road pattern was established so the local architects of the day were commissioned to design houses for the new prestigious estate. Evans and Jolley, of course, Samuel Dutton Walker and his nephew John Howitt, Arthur Brewill, Henry Sulley, W A Heazell and A H Goodall, were some of the first architects involved. The houses came in a steady stream through the 1880s and 1890s. As noted earlier, Colonel Wright engaged Evans and Jolley to design a new Lodge for the Hall, approval was granted on 21 August 1885. It stands with its forgotten crest on the corner of Mansfield Road and Mapperley Hall Drive. After William Lambert relinquished the lease of the Hall and about the time Colonel Wright and his son Charles Bingham Wright returned to take up residence, Evans and Jolley carried out alterations and additions at the Hall, 1889-90.

Whatever brief was given by clients to their architects the architects were bound by certain constraints set out in a large three page document 'Conditions of Sale of Portions of Mapperley Park and Lands, at Mapperley, in the Parish of Basford and County of Nottingham' ('County' was crossed out and 'extended Borough' written in which suggests the document was prepared before 1877). Throughout the 14 Sections the reserved rights of the Vendors are very clearly set down. It is sufficient here to quote the last section:

> XIV - The Lands sold will include one moiety in width of the Streets or Roads adjoining thereto respectively, and will be sold subject to such restrictions as to the Messuage or number of Messauges to be built thereon as will be agreed upon and specified in the Agreement for sale and purchase in each case respectively, and no other building than such one Messuage or such number of Messuages as will be so specified in the said Agreements respectively, with the necessary Stables, Coach Houses, and other out Offices thereto, shall be erected or built upon any part of such Land (except an entrance Lodge or Gardener's Cottage), and that each Messuage shall cost not less than £800 exclusive of Out-buildings, Fences, and Sewers, and shall be occupied as a private Dwelling-house only, and no part of any Land sold shall be used as a Brickyard or for the making or burning of bricks thereon, nor shall any such Messuage or Building be used as a School or public or private Asylum for Lunatics or Idiots or as a Hospital or as a House for Convalescents or as an Institution for any class of persons, nor shall any trade, business, or manufacture be carried on thereupon or any act or thing be done which may be or become a nuisance or noisy or offensive to the neighbourhood thereof, but the same shall be used as and for a private Dwelling-house only, and the said Land shall be used only as and for a Garden or Pleasure Ground or as Grass Land attached to such Messuage.

A

Arthur Brewill Architect Nottingham

B

A. H. Goodall Architect Nottingham N.° 5457

C 1

C 2

(C) *ELEVATION TO ZULLA RD*

D.

Mapperley Park houses by:

A) Arthur Brewill, Zulla Road North (1888)
B) A H Goodall, Radcliffe Road - Zulla Road (1887)
C) Arthur Brewill, Zulla Road - Ebers Road
        (1) 1889   (2) Revised 1890, note change of style!
D) W H Radford, Ebers Road (1900)

The Ordnance Survey 25 inch Map of 1901 shows almost all of the building work completed in Mapperley Park at the turn of the century. Missing are the first houses on Ebers Road, a pair, the first of four pairs, by W H Radford for himself, approval was given on 30 March 1900. One development north of Ebers Road was the acquisition by the Governors of the High School in the spring of 1897 of an area of some six acres for use as a playing field. This cricket ground was a rectangle near the centre of the plot of land situated between Ebers Road and the drive to Mapperley Hall, access was via a pathway from Mansfield Road. The playing field was slightly re-aligned after the area was sold for housing.[7] One interesting prelude to the second stage of the Mapperley Park Estate was the arrival of the electric tramway. The track was laid along Mansfield Road during 1899-1900. The stables of the earlier horse tram system, on the site of Carrington Lido, were closed and Sherwood Depot was opened in 1900, and after trials in November and December, the Sherwood route opened on 1 January 1901. A little later the route on the other side of the estate, along Woodborough Road to Porchester Road, was completed.

In 1900 C B Wright remained at the Hall, the Colonel is listed as living at Radcliffe Hall and Watcombe Park, Torquay, a residence he had purchased in September 1876 from the executors of I K Brunel for £23,000. He used it extensively from the late 1880s. It is just possible that Watcombe Circus, by Evans and Jolley 1874, is named after this house. The bank, I and I C Wright and Co, 1 Carlton Street to address it correctly, was rebuilt between 1888-1893. It was absorbed into the 'Capital and Counties Bank' in 1898, which later in 1918 became part of Lloyds Bank. By 1902 the Wright family had left the city, Colonel Charles Ichabod Wright died at Hantendale near Farnham, Surrey in 1905 aged 76. His son, C B, died in 1914 aged 60.

Early in 1903 Messrs Morris and Place were advertising the forthcoming sale by auction of the Mapperley Park Estate. In the Nottingham Daily Express of Thursday 19 March 1903 appeared the following:

SALE TOMORROW

A CHARMING FREEHOLD RESIDENTIAL ESTATE within the City Boundary of Nottingham and under a mile and a half from the centre of Nottingham known as Mapperley Hall, having extensive and exceedingly valuable frontages to the Mansfield Road, Woodborough Road and Lucknow Drive. The Hall has a southern aspect and stands in a good position commanding views of great beauty over the prettily laid out gardens, terraces and the magnificently timbered and undulating park and being approached by a carriage drive lined with an avenue of grand old trees with a pretty lodge entrance from the Mansfield Road.

The Estate will be offered for SALE by AUCTION by Messrs MORRIS AND PLACE at their Estate Sale Room 25 and 27 Bridlesmith Gate, Nottingham, on Friday, 20th day of March, 1903 at 3.30 o'clock and Subject to the Conditions of Sale as shall then be declared and also in the printed particulars.[8]

Notes

1   Later, the next generation of Wrights made a present of the ground and gave a substantial donation to the building fund for another church on the other side of the estate, St Jude's, Woodborough Road, designed by Evans and Jolley, 1877, but substantially altered by later additions. Colonel Wright gave the land for Carrington Vicarage.

2   Edward Manlove of Manlove, Alliott, Bloomsgrove Works, Ilkeston Road, Engineers and Machine Manufacturers.

3   Not available, perhaps deposited in a local solicitor's office. A plan, not seen, certainly is deposited.

4   William Lambert of W J and T Lambert and Co lace dressers and dyers, Lower Talbot Street (of Lambert's Factory).

5   Henry Smith Wright (1839(?)-1910) was MP for Nottingham South for nine years, 1886-1895.

6   Although some plans were deposited from 1871 the Compulsory Submission of plans for proposed buildings and the laying out of roads etc started on 4 September 1874.

7   The High School governors only secured a short lease on the playing field. In June 1899 they decided to purchase, but at the last minute the owner refused to sell. After the sale of the Mapperley Park Estate in 1903, a sale which included the playing field, it was essential that the future of the land, some six acres, be secured. Alderman Bright, one of the school governors, bought the land and offered it to the school at the price he paid £5,800. When the playing field was sold to Nottingham Corporation in the late 1920s the price had risen to £6,750. The High School moved to a larger site on Valley Road in 1931, and their old sports ground became the City Police Training Ground. With the police long gone the ground's future is uncertain and a source of anxiety for local residents.

8   Earlier advertising in the Nottingham Daily Express (14 March 1903) "The Estate ... its easy adaptability for immediately cutting up into building lots or for purchase by a public body or philanthropist for a public park offers such advantages that no other property in this area could be placed in the market to compete with it."

Ordnance Survey 25 inch map 1901 showing extent of building in Mapperley Park c 1899.

The Mapperley Park Estate c 1902 surveyed by
W B Starr possibly in preparation for its
auction on 20 March 1903.

Part Three

The sale of the northern portion of the Mapperley Park Estate duly took place, as advertised, on Friday 20 March 1903. The sale was forced upon the Wright family by a judgement of the High Court. At the end of October 1902, Capital and Counties Bank Limited brought an action against Colonel Charles Ichabod Wright, Mr Frederick Wright, Mr Charles Bingham Wright, of Nottingham, and Mr John William Davy, retired bankers, Mr Nevill Knight and Mr Francis John Carter, solicitor of Torquay. It was heard by Mr Justice Joyce in the Chancery Division. The Bank sought a declaration that they were entitled to a lieu on monies due under arrangements for the purchase by the plaintiffs from the first four defendants of a banking business four years earlier. The bank had been carried on by them in partnership at Nottingham under the name of I and C Wright.[1]

The plaintiffs also asked for the realisation and sale of the former bank's remaining assets. His lordship concurred and ordered a sale and realisation without prejudice. The Bank brought two other actions and by consent of the two parties Mr Justice Joyce directed a sale by the Court of certain securities given by two of the partners on the Mapperley and Basford Estates. Thus by the Judgement made on 10 November 1902, it was ordered that all hereditaments and premises listed in an indenture[2] of 8 February 1873, forming the Mapperley Park Estate:

> " ... as then still remained unsold be sold with the approbation of the Judge and that the money to arise by such sale be paid into Court to the credit of that action to an account to be entitled 'Proceeds of Sale of Mapperley Estate' subject to further order."

The sale of the remaining 'unsold' portion of the Mapperley Park Estate was an event of great interest and importance extending well beyond the city boundaries and was reported the next day in the Nottingham Daily Express:

> "Messrs Morris and Place auctioneers offered yesterday at their saleroom, Bridlesmith Gate, Nottingham, the well known freehold residential estate of Mapperley Hall. The estate which is within the city boundary and about 1½ miles from the Great Market Place, comprises the family mansion known as Mapperley Hall, together with the picturesque and finely timbered park lands containing 129 acres, 3 rods and 36 poles or thereabouts, lodge entrance, farmhouse and cottage and has frontages to the Mansfield Road, Woodborough Road and Lucknow Drive.

> The mansion[3], a substantial structure overlooking the Park and grounds with a south-east aspect, was recently occupied by Colonel C I Wright. The sale attracted a large influential gathering of gentlemen, the site being, as the auctioneer said, one of the very best available for prospective building purposes.

> The first bid offered was one of £60,000 by Mr F Acton, this being rapidly followed by increases of £1,000 until total of £70,000 was reached. Next followed two advances of £500 and then further increases until at £74,000 the hammer fell and the estate passed into the hands of Mr S P Derbyshire of Derbyshire Brothers, chartered accountants. Messrs Cameron, Kemm and G London were the vendors' solicitors."

Several pointed observations on the auction were made by the writer of the comment column elsewhere in the Nottingham Daily Express:

"On the whole I should say the purchasers of Mapperley Park Estate yesterday afternoon got a bargain, the purchase price being £74,500 being about 2s 6d a yard.

It is hardly a secret that Mr S P Derbyshire was acting for a syndicate and the Mayor and Mr Ball, I am told, were mutually interested in the bidding against Mr Derbyshire."

The Syndicate mentioned consisted initially of Job Nightingale Derbyshire, Samuel Patrick Derbyshire and John Ashworth. There might have been several others at the very least highly interested if not actually involved. The name of William Beedham Starr, a prominent local architect, was added, handwritten, soon after the sale to one of the earliest printed documents relating to the development of the estate. Thereafter, the developers were Ashworth, Derbyshire and Starr. Starr was an excellent, if obvious choice. He appears to have surveyed the Wright's estate for the auctioneers' sale catalogue and associated documents. From July 1903 onwards he was involved with plans and sections of Ebers Grove and the revision of plans for the eastern extension of Ebers Road, the last major roadworks on the earlier development. He also submitted designs of houses for a number of clients on these two roads.

By the spring of 1904 the master plan for the Mapperley Park Estate was ready. The original submission date of 16 April was put back to 12 May and then on 27 May 1904, the following plans were approved for Messrs Ashworth, Derbyshire and Starr, Mansfield Road.

1   Plans and Sections of new streets to be called Mapperley Hall Drive, Arlington Drive, Hatfield Road, Sefton Drive, Tavistock Drive, Tavistock Avenue, Lucknow Avenue, Carisbrooke Drive, Alverstone Road and Esher Grove.

2   Plan and Section of further length of Cyprus Road and new street to be called Carisbrooke Avenue.

Starr revised the plans for Arlington Drive in October and in November 1904. Early in February 1905 William Dymock Pratt put forward Plans and Sections of new streets, Richmond Drive extension, Warwick Road and Woodland Drive for the Derbyshire brothers. At first these plans were rejected because of incorrect street levels, however, after revision, approval was given on 24 February. On the same day Starr successfully submitted two sets of Plans and Sections of new streets on behalf of the Syndicate. The first was for continuation of Lucknow Avenue to Mapperley Hall Drive. The second was somewhat misleadingly listed as 'New streets to be called Lucknow Drive, Mapperley Hall Drive, Richmond Drive, Warwick Road and amended section of Sefton Drive'. In June 1905 the revised plans of Arlington Drive were altered yet again. Over a year later on 19 October 1906 Starr's extension of Mapperley Hall Drive to Woodborough Road was approved.

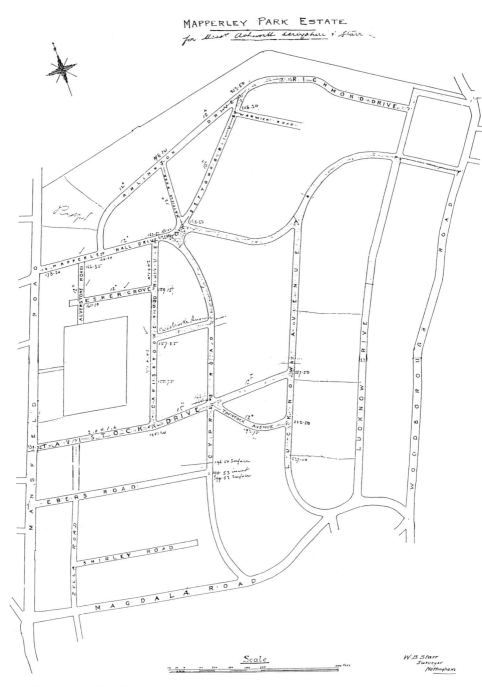

The plan showing the proposed development of the northern part of the Mapperley Park Estate submitted by W B Starr on 27 May 1904. A number of minor amendments were made later to this original layout.

To THE SURVEYOR OF THE LOCAL BOARD OR HEALTH, NOTTINGHAM,

SIR,

I do hereby give you Notice, That I intend to* set out the following
roads upon the Mapperley Park Estate,

Mapperley Hall Drive, Arlington Drive, Hatfield Road,
Lofton Drive, Tavistock Drive, Tavistock Avenue,
Lucknow Avenue, Caudebote Drive,
Wiverton Road and Esher Grove, for
Henry Ashworth, Derbyshire and Stan.

and herewith _____ have deposited at your Office (St. Peter's Church Side) a Plan and Section of such
intended "New Street," drawn to the Scales named, and accompanied with all the requirements
described in the 19th Clause of the above Bye-Laws.

And that _____ pay _____ of 12 St. Peters Gate Nott.

is to be the Surveyor and _____ to have charge of the Works to be laid out.

DATED this twelfth day of October 188-79— May 1904.

Signature, W.B. Starr

Address, 12 St. Peter Gate Nott.

BYE-LAWS, 1870.

BOROUGH OF NOTTINGHAM.

AS TO NEW STREETS.

NOTICE No. _____

Name, W.B. Starr

Address, 12 St. Peters Gate.

Date, April 16th 1904

ONE MONTH'S NOTICE to Borough Surveyor, as to
intention to lay out New Streets on the
Mapperley Park Estate.

Details of the planning application for the
development of the Northern Part of the
Mapperley Park Estate submitted by W B Starr.

Page 23

W B Starr and his office were heavily committed during the summer of 1904 on subdividing part of the estate into building plots of various sizes. By July 1904 a plan had been prepared showing that most plots in the area bounded by Mapperley Hall Drive, Cyprus Road, Ebers Road (north), Grosvenor Avenue, Tavistock Drive and Mansfield Road had been apportioned. A study of the plan reveals distinct groups of people involved. the names of several prominent townsmen appear as purchasers for investment for example John Dane Player and Joseph Bright, solicitor. Named also are the minor architect developers, the reoccurrence of whose names, later with submissions for groups of houses, shows the intention of speculative building.

F H Collyer and W B Savidge are typical of this group. A number of plots were taken by individuals, most of whom later had a very individual house, designed by Starr, erected on their investment. Members of the Syndicate also managed to acquire or hold onto a number of prime sites, either collectively or separately. Lastly, a few local builders, of no great architectural potential, tried to get a stake in the new estate. One or two succeeded.

The interest and activity generated by the exciting development prospects for the northern part of the estate tended to divert attention away from housing being put up in the area south and east of Ebers Road. At the same time the grounds of Forest House east of Mansfield Road and between Redcliffe and Mapperley Roads, adjoining the former road were opened up for new roads and housing. Forest House and its immediate surrounds had been given, together with monetary gifts to the Committee of the Children's Hospital by Thomas Isaac Birkin in 1899.

W H Radford followed his first pair of houses on Ebers Road with two other pairs before the end of 1900, and a third pair in August 1901 all adjoining on the original plot. Another pair by Radford, again on Ebers Road, was submitted and approved in March 1902. The only other activity in that period was on Shirley Road where F C Martin prepared plans for two pairs of houses for J G Martin in October 1900 and May 1901.

During 1902 and the first half of 1903, the major building works took place on the Forest House Estate mentioned earlier. On 26 September 1902, Robert Evans and Son's Plans and Sections for a new street off Redcliffe Road, Forest House Road were approved. The name was soon changed to Berkley Avenue. This was undertaken for T I Birkin and E A F Sankey. On 27 March 1903, for T I Birkin and others, Evans and Son presented Plans and Sections of new streets to be called Thorncliffe Road and Thorncliffe Rise. Finally Evans and Son, this time for T I Birkin and the architect surveyor A R Calvert, had their Plan and Section of a new street, Andrew Road, passed on 16 October 1903. Houses erected on these roads during the years 1902-4 included designs by Brewill and Baily, Hedley J Price, William Dymock Pratt, Lawrence Bright, W and R and F Booker, Calvert and Gleave, Harry Gill and T Long.

W B Starr's amended plan for part of Ebers Road and his Plans and Sections for Ebers Grove for G Sadler and others were approved on 24 July 1903, and re-submitted with deviations from the approved plans on 14 August 1903. This revived interest in the area and houses by Starr and Bright soon followed. Besides singles, pairs and threes, Starr designed 12 houses for H B Spencer in Ebers Grove and 14 houses for J Hutchinson on Mansfield Road and Ebers Road, both in March 1904. Bright's commissions included 13 houses on Ebers Grove for H Moore, both in

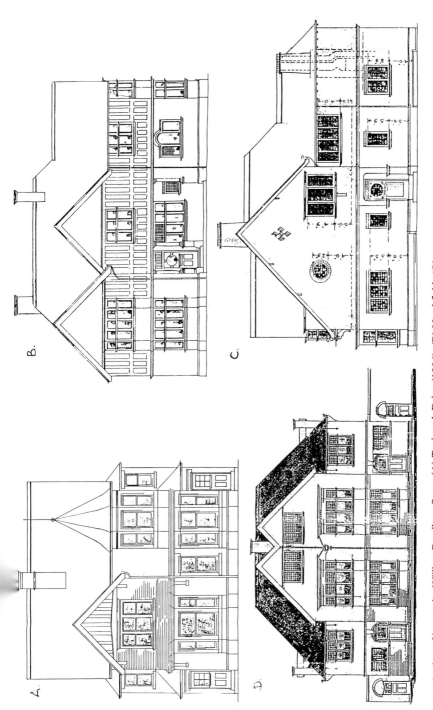

A selection of houses by William Beedham Starr: (A) Tavistock Drive (1906), (B) Northfield, 470 Mansfield Road, Starr's own house (1906), (C) Mapperley Hall Drive and Alverstone Road (1907), (D) Mapperley Hall Drive (1907).

May 1904. An unusual development was the block of 20 houses on Lucknow Avenue for A H Vass by the Long Eaton Architect J F Dodd approved on 27 May 1904. Albert Henry Vass lived in Musters Road, West Bridgford, was an official of the Ilkeston Brick Company and employed Long Eaton builders!

One terrible scheme for 56 houses, all virtually identical and of no great merit, was passed on 5 August 1904. It was submitted by A H Peel for J H Peel and was intended to cover much of the area bounded by Lucknow Avenue, Tavistock Avenue and Cyprus Road. J H Peel appears to have been a small-time joiner and undertaker living nearby at 578 Woodborough Road. The plans were badly drawn. The designated area was still awaiting its buildings when the Ordnance Survey Map of 1938 was being prepared. One can, of course, speculate why these houses were never built; perhaps the whole project was badly conceived lacking experience, expertise and finance. Perhaps some outside pressure or inducement was involved to thwart an intrusion which would certainly have inhibited the grandiose intentions of the Syndicate. J H Peel did successfully put forward proposals for nine houses outside the estate on Woodborough Road near Mission Street on 9 June 1905.

Elsewhere on the older part of Mapperley Park relatively few houses were put up between 1900 and 1904. On Redcliffe Road, Brewill and Baily designed two houses for F Action (1901) and Bright produced four for a Mr Ketton (1903). One house on Cyprus Road (1903) and two on Lucknow Drive (1904) came from the office of W D Pratt. The second of these, for S R Trotman, the city analyst, shows a much freer style suggesting an awareness of Charles Voysey[4]. Another house by F C Martin for J G Martin on Shirley Road (1903) and five houses by William Herbert Higginbottom for G Sadler on Cyprus Road completes the list of new building before the onset of activity on the newly laid out streets on the northern part of the estate.

The first planning application for Grosvenor Avenue and Tavistock Drive came, perhaps inevitably, from Starr; six houses for J W Moore submitted on 28 October 1904, but delayed by alterations and resubmitted on 3 March 1905. Throughout 1905 houses by Starr, F H Collyer, and Savidge and Collyer were approved for Tavistock Drive.

At the same time the first houses were being authorised for Richmond Drive by W D Pratt; Sefton Drive - Mapperley Hall Drive by A Glen; and at the end of 1905 Esher Grove - Alverstone Road by L Bright. The first houses on Carisbrooke Drive and Warwick Road received planning consent in the spring of 1906 designed by Savidge and Collyer and W D Pratt respectively.

It is about this time that William Beedham Starr starts to show his qualities as an extremely good designer of houses. He had started his own architectural practice some ten years earlier. Gradually he progressed from straightforward mundane jobs: converting four pail closets to wcs and 34 privies to wcs (1898) to a wide range of domestic, commercial and industrial commissions. He appears to have tackled anything, intermingling large and small assignments. In the wooded parkland on the northern part of the estate he certainly grasped his opportunities to produce a wide range of individually designed houses. His own house 'Northfield', 470 Mansfield Road, on the corner of Mapperley Hall Drive and facing the Lodge of the old estate, built in 1906, exemplifies this. Again, and to a much greater extent than W D Pratt's passing glance, he exhibits an affinity to the work of Voysey. Tucked away in this secluded area of Nottingham is a veritable treasure house of Edwardian domestic architecture.

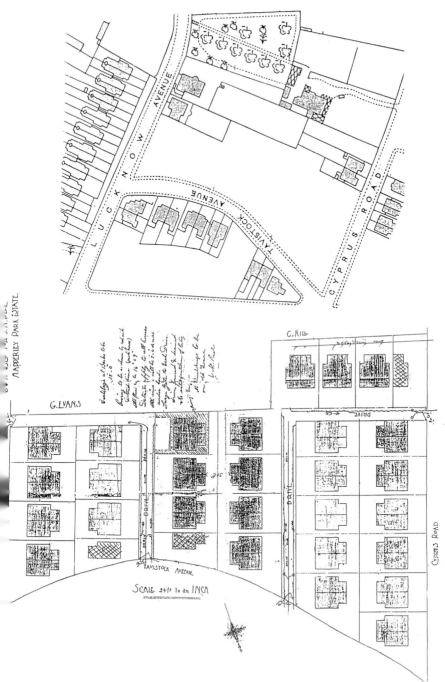

The ill conceived and unfulfilled estate of 56 houses prepared by A H Peel (1904), left. The plot, between Lucknow Avenue and Cyprus Road, remained largely empty long after the scheme was forgotten, (OS 1938), right.

Notes

1 The acquisition of I and C Wright's Bank by Capital and Counties Bank Limited took place in June 1898. The Capital and Counties Bank Limited paid £11,000 for: the goodwill of the (banking) business, the price of the premises to be as quoted in the books; arrangements for the taking over of the customers accounts and for the local directorships. They paid a further £96,747-16-10d for the bank's investment portfolio. Frederick and Charles Bingham Wright were appointed as local directors of the Capital and Counties Bank.

2 The indenture of 8 February 1873 was made between C I Wright, H S Wright, F Wright, G H Wright, the Hon Theodosia Wright and Charles Augustus Welby. A further indenture was made on 15 May 1900 between C I Wright, and N Wright and F J Carter (thereby designated Trustees).

3 Mapperley Hall was very well appointed. The principal rooms on the ground floor were the dining room 44ft 6in by 19ft 6in; the drawing room 29ft by 23ft 6in; the music room, whose ceiling was 'painted by an eminent artist', 34ft 6in by 17ft 6in; and the library 27ft by 10ft. On the first floor, mainly, there were 20 bedrooms; three dressing rooms and many other rooms, including 'ample linen cupboards, store rooms and boxrooms'. On the second floor there was a billiard room 29ft 6in by 16ft 6in with an adjoining smokers' lounge. Elsewhere there was a servants' hall 21ft by 15ft plus butler's pantry and plateroom and kitchen housekeeper's room. The basement contained a game larder, two wine cellars, two beer cellars and a cool cellar.

Close to the Hall fronting an open courtyard was a coach house for seven carriages, and a coach wash-house; a four stall stable and six loose boxes. Nearby was a coachman's cottage, over the stable was a dormitory for four lads. There was a blacksmith's shop and a painter's shop.

In the kitchen garden were three vineries, two melon houses, a lean-to cucumber house, and a pineapple pit which was heated by steam pipes. The fruit garden had three summer houses.

There was a farm cottage with two bedrooms, etc; an open courtyard with cart-shed, harness room, rock beer cellar, barn, an open loft granary and carpenter's shop. There were standings for 34 cows in six cow sheds plus two calf sheds and a large stack yard in the rear. The minerals and the timber were included in the sale.

4 Charles Voysey (1857-1941) built a large number of modestly proportioned country houses between c 1890-1914. He respected the rural tradition of English architecture without slavishly attempting to recreate it. Some facets of his style may be seen in Edwardian Mapperley Park.

Mapperley Hall 1881.

West Elevation.

Mapperley Hall showing the alterations of 1889-90 prepared by the Nottingham architectural practice of Robert Evans and William Jolley. "Viewed" across the former Police Sports Ground, Mansfield Road.

Mapperley Hall appears not to have attracted local artists. Engravings, drawings, even old photographs of the building seem to be non-existent. In one or two old sepia photographs of Mapperley Park the eye of faith can discern a small fragment of what could be a very large house!

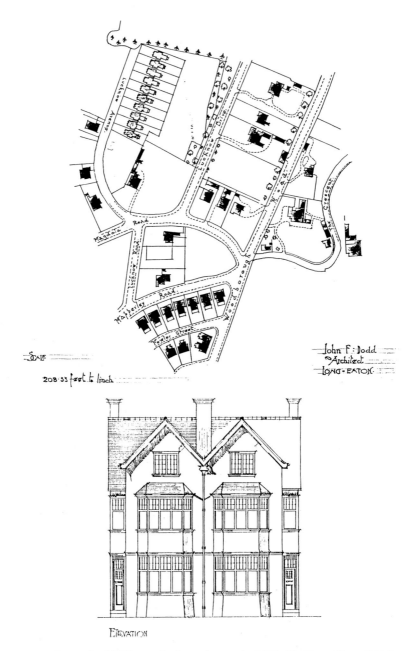

Twenty Houses for A H Vass on Lucknow Avenue, by J F Dodd of Long Eaton (1904).

Part Four

Sixteen houses were approved in the second half of 1906 for the northern portion of the Mapperley Park Estate. That made a total of 38 houses for 1906, all in the area sold at auction in 1903, approximately lying between Mansfield Road and Woodborough Road and northwards from Ebers Road to the fringe of Private Road. Between 1906 and the outbreak of the First World War in August 1914, some 163 houses received planning consent. Only one house, that for A Hemsley between Redcliffe Road and Magdala Road designed by W D Pratt in 1909 was in the older part. This house was rather unusual in that its outbuildings included stables and a coach house with flat, whilst neighbours were already opting for motor houses!

In detail the pattern of approved new houses:

1906	38 houses of these		5 by W B Starr			
1907	32 "	"	15 "			
1908	33 "	"	7 "			
1909	14 "	"	5	W B Starr/Starr and Hall		
1910	20 "	"	2	W B Starr/W B Starr and E B H Hall		
1911	15 "	"	-	"		
1912	8 "	"	2	"	"	"	"
1913	-		-			
1914	_3_ "	"	_3_	"	"	"	"
	163 "		39			

Of the 39 houses by Starr or Starr and Hall 13 were built for Starr and two for Hall. Of the other houses 39 were designed by W B Savidge and F H Collyer, either individually or together. Twentyeight of these were for Collyer and Co. Whereas Starr built seven pairs of houses Savidge and Collyer's total included one eight, one six, one five and one three. In general Starr designed for individual clients whereas the bulk of Savidge and Collyer's work appears speculative.

Other architects well represented in this period are Lawrence Bright and Son (17 houses), A R Calvert and W R Gleave (10), W D Pratt (10), E A Sudbury (6). Several other well known local architects or builders who submitted plans for at least one house included H E Woodsend, T Long, H H Goodall, Sutton and Gregory, Heazell and Son and A E Lambert.

Whilst all of these new houses were being erected on the new roads, in the older part of the estate many houses were receiving alterations and additions. A number of motor garages or motor houses were put up, their building line often raising questions. In some of the newer houses a garage was incorporated, in others it was added later.

The very last entry in the Planning Books for the Mapperley Park Estate before the outbreak of war came on 31 July 1914, W D Pratt put forward plans for a greenhouse and potting shed for A Schmidt, Esq!

The area around Mapperley Hall was the one part of the estate that did not initially attract any attention. It would appear that the Derbyshire brothers and W B Starr, by an indenture of partition dated 12 July 1904, released their claims on the Hall, leaving its future in the hands of John Ashworth the other partner in the Syndicate. On 17 January 1905, Ashworth made an

Houses by W B Starr: (A) Alverstone Road and Esher Grove (1907), (B) Ebers Road (1907), (C) Alverstone Rod (1907), (D) Carisbrooke Drive (1908).

Calvert and Gleave
Mapperley Hall Drive (1910)

F H Collyer
Carisbrooke Drive (1911)

agreement with Nottingham Corporation whereby the Corporation agreed to purchase the Hall, together with part of its grounds, 13,000 yards, for the purpose of using the Hall as a men's hostel for University College, Nottingham.

The purchase price was £3,400, considered by some to be very little more than the cost of the land. The University College, granted a Charter of Incorporation in 1903, was at this time just down the road on part of what is now the Nottingham Trent University site.

On 10 June 1910 E A Sudbury submitted plans and sections of two new streets between Mapperley Hall Drive and Lucknow Avenue to be called Fifth and Sixth Avenues. This application, made on behalf of 'Major' Ashworth, was disapproved because of the width of the streets. The amended plans and sections were approved on 2 September 1910 but were never carried out. The development of the area still concerned Ashworth and on 15 August 1913 G C Cuthbert proposed on Ashworth's behalf plans and sections of three new roads. Two, Netley Avenue and Beaulieu Avenue, went from Mapperley Hall Drive approximately towards the Hall grounds aligned parallel to Lucknow Avenue. The third, Romsey Avenue, also parallel to Lucknow Avenue, ran from Tavistock Avenue to the older part of the estate. In addition a large number of building plots were marked out. Once again nothing came of the scheme, perhaps this time war intervened; the sites were still undeveloped in 1938. A short road between Alverstone Road and Carisbrooke Drive, linking Mapperley Hall Drive with Esher Grove, appeared on an early plan as Osborne Grove, but in fact it remained an unnamed track until it was divided up in the 1920s.

The presence of the cricket and sports field belonging to the Nottingham High School for boys established a sporting side to the estate; for a number of houses bordering the field their often splendid rear elevation was noted on plans as 'Elevation to Cricket Ground'.

A second tennis club, following the earlier Magdala Tennis Club, was formed at the courts at the corner of Mapperley Hall Drive and Carisbrooke Drive. On an original plan prepared by Starr c 1904-5 this 'Tennis Courts Area' is under the names of J H Shipstone, T E Beecroft and E B H Hall.

E B H Hall is the architect who later formed a partnership with Starr in the summer of 1909. Little is known of his career, but he certainly purchased some good sites, especially in Esher Grove at an early stage. His last assignment before joining Starr was the conversion of four dwellinghouses into saleshops for A G Foss on Loscoe Road, not far away, in April 1909.

As the war clouds gathered to blot out the late Edwardian sun, the nature of the Mapperley Park Estate was well established. A certain elegant comfortable and spacious lifestyle had been created for over 200 families on the wooded parkland around the old family home of Wrights the Bankers.

William Beedham Starr must receive belated credit for its creation. As has been shown, he prepared the original master plan; through the syndicate who purchased the land he imposed standards and with no little architectural flair he produced a stream of distinctive houses. The role of the architect in the evolution of Victorian and Edwardian Nottingham has been long neglected.

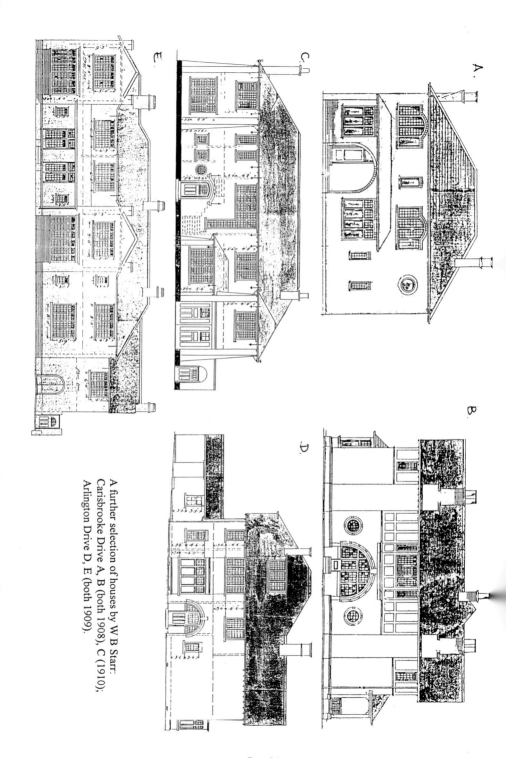

A further selection of houses by W B Starr: Carisbrooke Drive A, B (both 1908), C (1910); Arlington Drive D, E (both 1909).

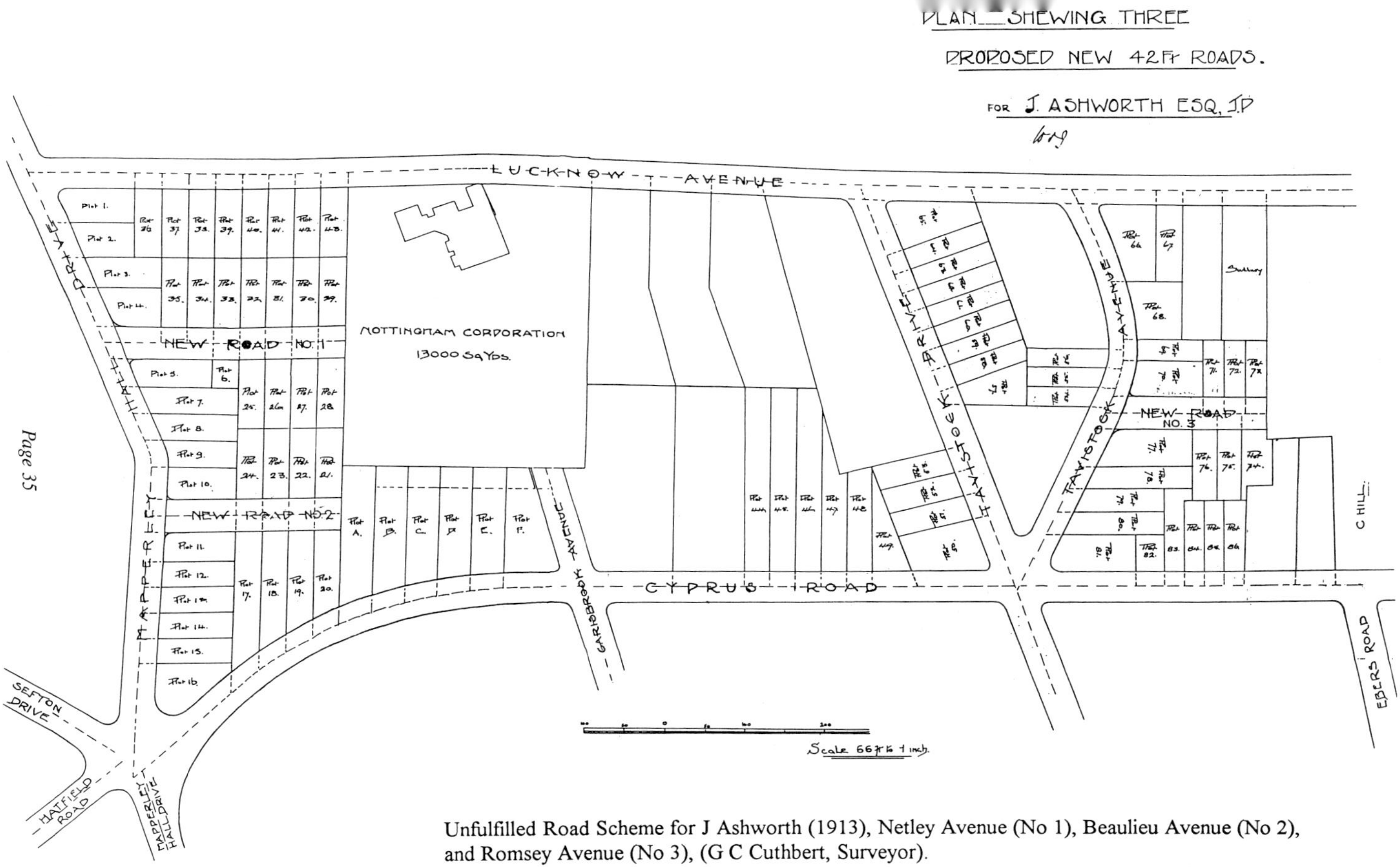

PLAN SHEWING THREE
PROPOSED NEW 42 Ft ROADS.
FOR J. ASHWORTH ESQ, J.P.
LUCKNOW AVENUE
HALL DRIVE
MAPPERLEY
NEW ROAD NO. 1
NEW ROAD NO. 2
NEW ROAD NO. 3
NOTTINGHAM CORPORATION
13000 Sq Yds.
GARIBROOK AVENUE
CYPRUS ROAD
TAVISTOCK DRIVE
TAVISTOCK AVENUE
EBERS ROAD
C HILL
SEFTON DRIVE
HATFIELD ROAD
MAPPERLEY HALL DRIVE
Scale 66 ft to 1 inch.

Unfulfilled Road Scheme for J Ashworth (1913), Netley Avenue (No 1), Beaulieu Avenue (No 2), and Romsey Avenue (No 3), (G C Cuthbert, Surveyor).

Much had been achieved in a little over ten years yet a sizeable area remained untouched. Very little building had taken place in the parallelogram formed by Tavistock Drive, Lucknow Avenue, Mapperley Hall Drive and Carisbrooke Drive. Other roads still had a few plum sites available.

The Corporation purchased Mapperley Hall and rented it to the Council of the University College. During the First World Ward the Mapperley Hall Hostel was transformed into a V A D Auxiliary Hospital, accommodating sixty patients. Possession of the Hall reverted to the College in 1919. It remained a men's hostel until the outbreak of the Second World War, when, with a shrinking intake of men students, the College Council decided to close Mapperley Hall as a hostel. In April 1940 the building became the headquarters of Number 3 (North Midland) Region for Civil Defence. A special war room for the control of the regional defence services was created in the grounds. It was the nerve centre of the regional defence organisation for the rest of the war.

For sometime after the war the Hall was used by the Electricity Board. In 1974 the Severn Trent Water Authority started to share the building. Finally in 1976 the Electricity Board moved out leaving the Water Authority as sole occupants. Their staff were relocated in 1990 leaving the building empty except for a caretaker who remained for another three years. The Hall and its grounds were finally sold off for development on 4 August 1995. The local fear is that such a prominent site could be onverdeveloped.

[In passing, it is worth noting that in Lenton Hall, another former home of one of the bankers of the Wright family, was purchased as a second men's hostel. This was much closer to the University College, now at Highfields.]

The original change of use of the Hall in 1906 from a private house to a hall of residence for a University College might have breached existing covenants. These covenants restricted the use of "buildings or intended buildings as schools or institutions for any class of person". In fact, the consortium, together with J D Player and Alderman J Bright owners of adjoining property raised no objections to the establishment of a student hostel.

Elsewhere in the list of covenants there is one forbidding the setting up of " .. hospital or home for convalescents". All buildings should be " ... for the purpose of a private dwellinghouse or for domestic purposes ..." Further " ... all houses which should at any time be built upon the said piece or parcel of land should be detached or semi-detached and should cost not less than £500 for each single house and £650 for each pair of semi-detached houses including the outoffices and premises portaining thereto."

W D Pratt, Magdala - Redcliffe Roads (1909)

ELEVATION of STABLES

Suitable premises have been offered forming that portion of the Mapperley Park Estate which comprises the Hall and about 13,000 yards of land including therein the site of the Hall.

Negotiations have been entered into with the owner, and a Contract of Sale and Purchase has been signed (subject to the approval of the Council), for the acquisition of the Hall and the land before-mentioned at the price of £3,400.

Your Committee understand from the Council of the College that the Hall, with some alterations, will form an excellent Hostel.

Such alterations will be carried out by the College.

The College will pay to the Corporation a net annual rental equal to $3\frac{1}{2}$ per cent. on the purchase money.

A separate Report from the College Council as to the necessity of the Hostel as a means of developing the usefulness of the College, and as to the costs of its maintenance is contained in the Appendix hereto.

Your committee have had the property valued by Messrs. Heazell & Son who report as follows:—

We are of opinion that the purchase price of £3,400 at which the property is offered is fair and reasonable, and we consider it a good investment for this sum. We are further of opinion that this land will increase in value as time goes on. The buildings have cost many thousands of pounds to erect, they are in fair condition, and a large portion could be utilised.

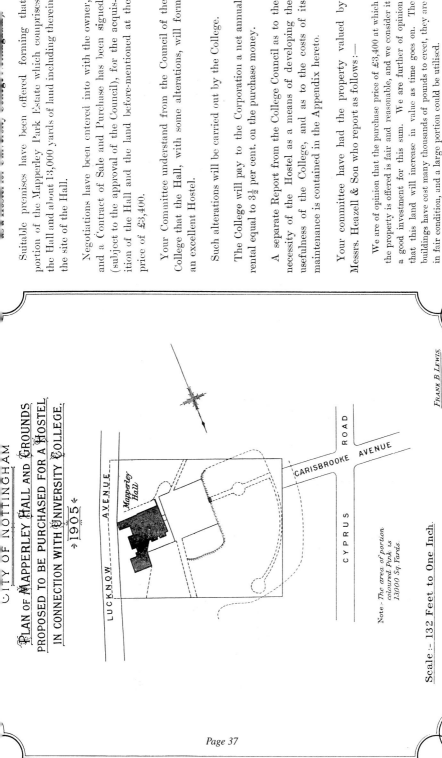

CITY OF NOTTINGHAM

PLAN OF MAPPERLEY HALL AND GROUNDS
PROPOSED TO BE PURCHASED FOR A HOSTEL
IN CONNECTION WITH UNIVERSITY COLLEGE.

÷1905÷

LUCKNOW AVENUE

Mapperley Hall

CARISBROOKE AVENUE

CYPRUS ROAD

Note:- The area of portion
coloured Park is
13000 Sq.Yards

Scale :- 132 Feet to One Inch.

FRANK B LEWIS,
City Architect,
25 / 1905

T. FORMAN & SONS, NOTTINGHAM, LONDON & GLASGOW

Part Five

The extent of the Mapperley Park Estate has always been confined to the Wrights' land bounded by Mansfield Road to the west, Woodborough Road to the east, the Duke of Newcastle's land (the gardens of Private Road) to the north and Redcliffe Road to the south. William Beedham Starr's plans for the layout of the estate approved in May 1904, together with the existing roads of the first phase of development from 1875, reached to the limited of the estate. Thus all later roads were extensions of existing roads or provided access to building plots so far undeveloped.

It has become fashionable to designate 'Mapperley Park' the area developed largely on the grounds of the old Forest House*, between Mapperley Road and Redcliffe Road and extending back from Mansfield Road. The early development of this area has already been noted. Twenty houses were built on this land between 1914-39 inclusive, nine of these went up to Thorncliffe Road in 1915.

Between 1914 and 1939 only two planning applications were made for new road works. On 4 July 1924, the architects Bright and Thoms, acting for E W Robinson and others , received approval for the extension of Carisbrooke Avenue. A T Sadler, on behalf of Sadler and Hole, submitted 'Plans and Section of a New Street to be called Regent Drive' on 18 May 1928. Approval was given but the actual date of construction is not apparent, however, on 9 March 1934, the name of the new street was altered to Old Hall Drive. Soon afterwards on 23 March 1934, the architects Calvert and Jessop deposited plans for the first house on "The Old Hall Drive." It may be recalled that Arthur R Calvert was involved with the very first roads in Mapperley Park.

What is quite remarkable is the variety of building that took place in the Mapperley Park Estate between the wars. Although the period under review is nominally from September 1914, no new houses were built during the First World War. The first post-war house was on Woodland Drive. The architect was A E Lambert, the architect of Nottingham's Albert Hall. The plans were passed on 21 March 1919. In the 20 year span, 1919-1939, just over 200 houses were built in the Park. The exact figure depends on whether or not houses on the Mansfield Road boundary are included.

The variety comes from the fact that the work of some 62 architects was approved and largely built. Thirtyseven architects are represented by just one house each! In addition the only purpose-built flats, a block of four on Cyprus Road, is all that came from the practice of Evans, Clarke and Woollatt. Robert Evans Senior, together with his partner William Jolley were prominent in the very first attempts to develop the estate.

Some of the eminent local architects of the day designed five or more of the Mapperley houses: Bright and Thoms (16 houses 1921-39), W R Gleave (12, 1922 mostly - 1929), Starr and Hall (11, 1922-35), H A Dickman (11, 1923-37). W A Kneller (1922-24) A E Eberlin (1922-25), D M Thorpe (1924-38), and Booker and Shepherd (1930) each produced five houses.

---

* Earlier known as the Victoria Park Estate or Patchett's Park after Edwin Patchitt, twice Mayor of Nottingham, Clerk to the Inclosure Commissioners, etc who lived at Forest House for many years from c 1850.

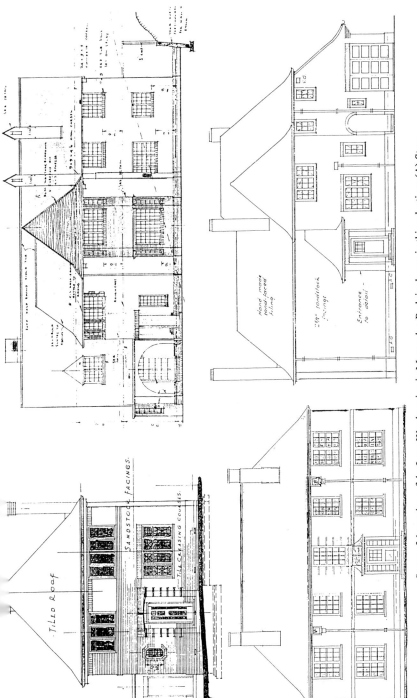

Some of the variety of the Inter-War housing in Mapperley Park is shown in this selection: (A) Starr and Hall, Carisbrooke Avenue (1933), (B) C F W Haseldine, The Point, Richmond Drive and Warwick Road (1933), (C) Evans, Clarke and Woollatt, Block of Four Flats, Cyprus Road (1907), (D) Thomas Long and Sons Ltd (R A Young, Architect), Mapperley Hall Drive, the last house approved before the Second World War (14 July 1939).

Quite outstanding on numbers alone was the contribution of Nehemiah Rigley. Initially Rigley was in partnership with Alex Wilson, their office was at 13 St Peter's Gate. They had a house erected on Thorncliffe Road and a house for themselves on Woodland Drive, both dated 1924. Then between January 1927 and November 1936 Rigley, now parted from Wilson and designing mainly for himself, built 58 houses. They are located on Shirley Road, Cyprus Road, Zulla Road, Redcliffe Road, Tavistock Avenue, Tavistock Drive, Lucknow Avenue and Carisbrooke Drive. It does appear that he made a point of acquiring a number of undeveloped sites in the older part of the estate.

Very little is known of Rigley. He is not listed in Kelly's 1925 Directory, except as a partner of Wilson. By 1928 he is living at 25 Shirley Road, perhaps in one of his own houses. His practice was a 5 St Peter's Church Walk. In the 1932 Kelly's Directory, Rigley is at 54 Cyprus Road the plans of which he had approved on 10 January 1930. His office has moved to Exchange buildings East. There is no mention of Rigley in the 1941 Directory, although he was preparing planning applications as late as 1939 for work in other parts of the city.

Besides the new houses a large number of the older houses were altered and extended. Many garages were built. Some of the work was undertaken by small builders but often the more notable architects of the day were engaged to prepare plans for 'Alterations and Additions' and for garages.

A significant feature of the changing social pattern started on 27 August 1937, when Thomas Long and Sons Ltd produced plans to divide 29 Tavistock Drive into two flats. This was approved, as was their subsequent 'Deviation from Approved Plans' submitted on 22 October 1937, whereby the number of flats was increased to three.

Only three further house to flats conversations were approved in the period up to January 1940. This last assignment, strictly outside the review period, was carried out by the noted architect T Cecil Howitt at 7 Arlington Drive. Howitt, perhaps best remembered for the Council House and his enlightened council housing of the 1920s, actually moved his practice from Exchange Buildings East to the corner of Mapperley Road and Mansfield Road in 1938. (Plans approved 14 November 1937).

Two quite distinctive, yet quite different, buildings were erected in the Park in the thirties. One was the new Sports Pavilion for the Magdala Lawn Tennis Club by Simms, Sons and Cooke Ltd, February 1936. The other was a Splinter Proof Shelter at Northwood, Arlington Drive, designed by Eberlin and Derbyshire, surprisingly, in July 1938.

Such a note of diversity, with its hint of another world conflict to come, seems to be a convenient point at which to end this resumé of the continuing development of Mapperley Park.